DAVID NASH

FULL CIRCLE

YORKSHIRE SCULPTURE PARK

Contents

Page 6
David Nash in conversation with Sir Peter Murray CBE, Founding Director, Yorkshire Sculpture Park

Page 26
On Drawing
David Nash

Page 29
Full Circle: David Nash and Drawing
Sarah Coulson
Curator, Yorkshire Sculpture Park

Page 34
The Weston Gallery
Exhibition photography by Jonty Wilde

Page 38
Lines and Smudges
David Nash

Page 41
Making Marks with the Subject's Material
David Nash

Page 49
Working with Trees
David Nash

Page 60
The Bothy Gallery
Exhibition photography by Jonty Wilde

Page 84
List of works

Page 88
Colophon

Previous double page: David Nash in his drawing studio, January 2022
Opposite: detail of pastels in the studio. Photographs: Jonty Wilde

David Nash in conversation with
Sir Peter Murray CBE, Founding Director,
Yorkshire Sculpture Park

Running Table, 1981, pictured with the artist's
Morris Shooting Brake. Photograph: David Nash

Peter Murray
David, we've known each other for so long. I've watched your work develop and evolve, and you've observed my work here at YSP. Although we will only touch the surface here, it's extraordinary what you have achieved over the years. I think the philosophical development of YSP, to a certain extent, kept pace with the philosophical evolution of your work, which might be an interesting place to start.

David Nash
1979 was when I first came to YSP. I'd done a residency at Grizedale the year before. Then the film *Woodman* was made by Peter Browne, funded by the Arts Council, and then you appeared. You got in touch with me so I came over, and I think this was when you invited me to be in a group show that you were planning.

PM
Yes, you were passing from Grizedale and you popped in. You had a Morris Shooting Brake with a piece of David Nash sculpture on the back holding it together.

DN
I'd repaired some of the wood on the car with an ash that still had a little branch on it.

PM
It was like a kinetic sculpture! It was a terrific meeting and we seemed to get on straight away. You next came back later in 1979 for the exhibition called *Wood*, which included many artists. You wanted to work on site, which I welcomed, and you found what you described as a "doomed tree".

DN
I was very into serendipity. When I drove into the Park I saw a tree with a big branch that had fallen off and I thought "perfect", but it was in the wrong place. I remember you were there at the behest and the permission of Bretton Hall College, using their grounds, and they had put down rules about which areas you could use. You were wonderfully ambivalent about my making this piece – I think you recognised the potential of the idea and decided to take a chance on the College's reaction. That's been your method and I think that's enabled you to create YSP as it is today.

PM
It wasn't easy in the early days for Yorkshire Sculpture Park. Fortunately, the Principal, Alyn Davies, was very much on my side, but there was quite a lot of opposition from some students and staff, so the *Square Nest* that you went on to make in that damaged tree was a brave, bold move on many counts because it ventured into an area that in theory we weren't allowed to use. Of course, that didn't bother the young David Nash who got his ladder out, straight up the tree with a chainsaw and within a few hours a masterpiece appeared. There was a crudeness, a bravado, about it, which significantly contributed to the power of that piece, and it has stayed in my mind almost as much as any other you've made. To me, that was not only an incredibly important sculpture in terms of your development, but also in terms of the Park. It was the first site-specific piece, and like a number of site-specific pieces made in those early days, it disappeared.

DN
You were ultimately saved the problem of it being in the wrong place by the tree falling over! That is typical of a mature beech – I only learned later that beech tend to have a central trunk with a crown of very big limbs and they grow in balance but there is a weakness in the crown because water lingers inside that space among the branches and they tend to rot. So when a big branch like that comes off the whole tree is out of balance and, inevitably, once that happens, it just falls apart. That was another bit of serendipity, because we had our flourish and I had done

Top: *Square Nest*, 1979
Bottom: *Square Nest* at YSP in 1979. Photograph: David Nash

what I wanted to do, and you didn't have to worry about it because it was gone. Perfect scenario.

PM
Indeed. We had to grasp opportunities wherever they presented themselves and try to make the most of what we had. We corresponded a lot at that time and I seem to remember in the early days that much of it was to do with money, which reflected the limited resources we were both working with.

DN
Yes, I'm a little embarrassed about that, but at that time I was just getting by on whatever I could. I was teaching around the country as a visiting lecturer and whenever I had a show, I would try to get expenses to cover me because my income was so low.

PM
I didn't mention it to make you embarrassed, but to reflect on the way things have changed, both for you and for YSP. I recently looked back through our archival material and your insurance prices for the works in the exhibition ranged from £20 to £200 and we had to have a whip round at this end to try and find the funds for that. It's also interesting to think about the point at which you actually decided to become a full-time artist, and how you managed to support yourself and your family financially. It was a huge risk in terms of how to keep the wolves away from the door.

DN
My aspiration was to be self-employed and to be free. In those early days, even before going to Chelsea College of Art, I realised I needed to keep my overheads low – so, don't have a mortgage and don't pay rent. Buying Capel Rhiw for £200 satisfied those two principles and we didn't need a big income, so that gave me much more time. We had just enough.

PM
I remember from previous discussions that discovering Constantin Brancusi was a turning point for you in terms of your approach.

DN
I was 16, I think, when I first heard about Brancusi. It was his lifestyle, the fact that he lived in his studio, that was the greatest inspiration. I was very impressed when I read stories about how he prepared his own bronzes, so he had a kiln in his studio to make the ceramic moulds. He'd cook dinner in there for his friends and at the end of the dinner his party piece was to scrape all the plaster off the table with a wire brush so everyone got covered in plaster dust.

PM
It's fascinating how art becomes a way of life. To an extent YSP became a way of life for me. You just spoke about Brancusi and making food, and I remember having many barbecues with you over the years. We cooked food here for your Fellowship opening at YSP in 1982; it was huge, and to me that was part of the process, part of the exhibition. Even the charring and the fire of the barbecue seemed to relate to your practice. At that time you also made some tree planting works, but we didn't manage to save the trees from the rabbits and squirrels.

DN
Yes, the larch planting. Everything was against it working, but in those days I was over optimistic. The soil was all wrong as it's clay, and I don't think there were any other larches growing in the area. I should have noticed that

PM
You say you were over optimistic. I would say you were incredibly determined.

DN
It's similar. You want something to happen, so you try to make it happen, but nature

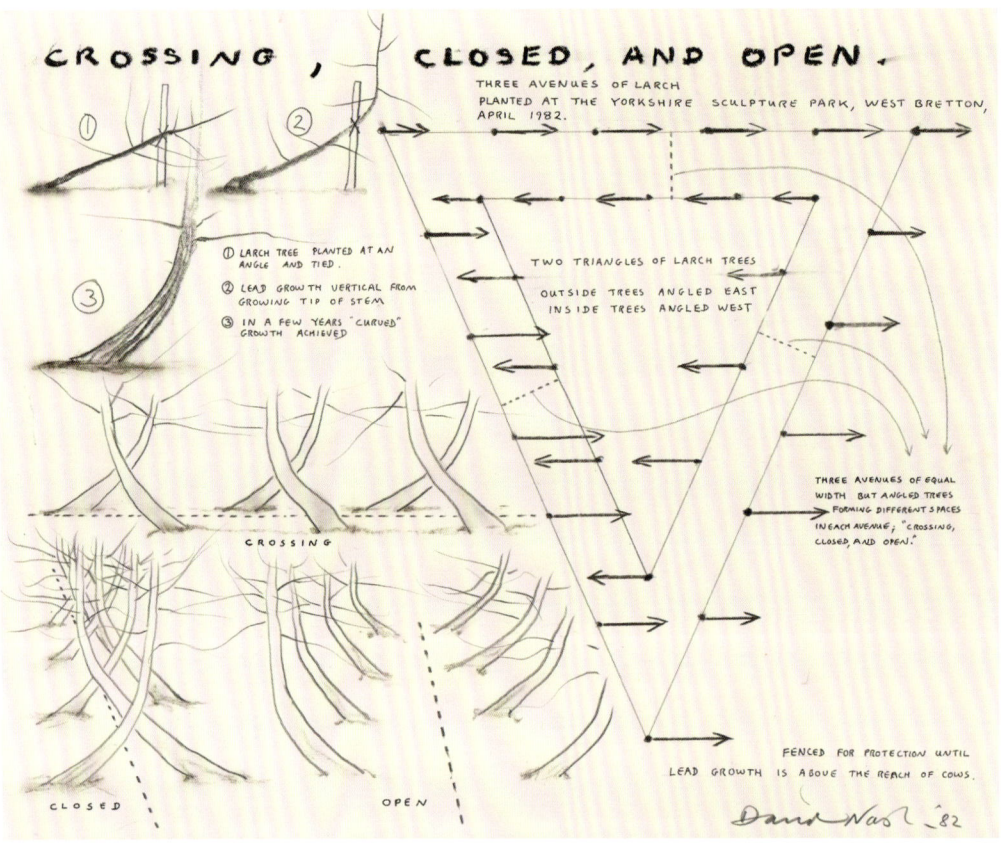

Top: *Crossing, Closed and Open*, 1982
Bottom: *Crossing, Closed and Open* being planted at YSP in 1982. Photograph: David Nash

deals with you, it teaches you. It says, "no, that doesn't work, but this would work".

PM
Hindsight is a wonderful thing, and in many ways I'm glad that those tree plantings didn't work.

DN
Me too. The idea was too contrived.

PM
It also led to a much stronger statement and a greater understanding on your part in terms of how to use planting as part of a work of art, and we will come on to your more recent tree planting later in this conversation. But first let's go back to the Fellowship. You'd always been busy and trying to correspond with you could be difficult because you were travelling around the world, or at least travelling around Europe. The Fellowship was interesting because it was broken down into sections, and there was one section where you were more or less permanently planted at YSP. You had your family here and your children went to school in West Bretton.

DN
The Fellowship was a very important year. I was on site at YSP from September through to December. I had already done a wood quarry in Maentwrog, with the tree that the *Wooden Boulder* came from, but I'd made that over two years. YSP was the first time that I'd worked continually with one tree in one place, because I had to teach, I had family, and so the fact that we could bring the family to Yorkshire Sculpture Park was really important. I was really pushing for something better than we had at Grizedale, and you found us a really nice house nearby in Sandal, which was brilliant. It was the fact that there was financial support, but also how sympathetic and enthusiastic you were that made it really possible. I felt a little guilty that I was getting paid by Yorkshire Sculpture Park for a year, as I was only there fully in residence for those few months. All the same, I did come back a lot; I remember staying in student accommodation.

PM
Yes, you came back and you did a project in Ilkley and in other places. I remember you sleeping on our front room floor on a couple of occasions too. I was beginning to learn how to deal with bureaucrats and administrators and politicians, so I saw it as a breath of fresh air. Your frenetic activity and travel brushed off on the creative spirit of YSP, and often when you went somewhere you established new contacts for us. It was a very significant period and an important Fellowship for YSP. I also think it cemented your long-term relationship with the Park, and we remained in continuous contact in one form or another. We also kept bumping into each other in different places around the world. It revealed to me how working with an artist over a longer period of time can be extremely mutually beneficial.

DN
I was very grateful for that. I remember Graham Beale came to visit me while I was working at YSP as he was keen on my work – he was Director of the San Francisco Museum of Modern Art. It was snowing when he came and he saw the wood quarry *20 Days with an Elm*. That visit actually transpired into my being involved with *A Quiet Revolution* that toured the States in 1987. Then there was the International Sculpture Conference that I was part of in 1983, which gave YSP real credence. People from Hakone Open-Air Museum were there, and it resulted in you and I getting an invitation to Japan the following year. Another important connection was with Rudi Oxenaar, and that led to me making a show at Kröller-Müller in The Netherlands, where he was Director.

PM
Yes, that was a really good connection, and by that time Rudi had become a Trustee of YSP.

DN

It was brilliant. The Dutch government had cut their support for the arts and cut the budget for the Kröller-Müller and so Rudi saw this as a good way to have an economic show. He was a supporter of my work but it was 1982, I was 36 or 37, so very young to be doing a whole one-person show, it was an incredible opportunity.

PM

The wood quarry you created at Kröller-Müller was, I believe, strongly influenced by *20 Days with an Elm*.

DN

Oh, yes, very much so. I went on for 15 years doing projects like that around the world, because it became very popular with museums. It was more economic because they didn't have to borrow work and then bring it over to Japan or America for example. They also got a lot of publicity because I was working there, so visible to the press. It ticked a lot of boxes, and it made me work in a way that meant I couldn't afford to hesitate. I had to find some way of getting out of prevaricating, which is what I used to do, just standing looking at this thing I was making, utterly bewildered about which way to go because there were so many possibilities.

PM

One of the things that you mention in relation to your work is getting to know wood better. Something I learned from my experience of working with you, but particularly from the Fellowship, was the way that you sensed the core of the material you were working with, and the way that you would take something which was doomed and give it a new existence, a new way of life. Working on *20 Days with an Elm* was an incredibly productive period for you in this respect, working in so many different ways with and around one fallen tree.

DN

For a lot of the drawings I did of *20 days with an Elm*, I used earth which came from digging out lumps of clay from around the roots, and I was exploring making works on paper from the process of my making sculpture. While looking through my works on paper for this current exhibition, I found a triangular scorch on a piece of paper, which is shown in the Bothy Gallery. When I dug to excavate the tree root, I found that the shape that was predominating was the triangle – or as a volume a pyramid – which is what I used right the way through that whole tree. So, I cut a three-sided hole down a log, put a fire at the bottom and when it was going nicely, I put a piece of paper on top of the log and it scorched in that triangle and flared a bit. It wasn't made using a printing press, it was made using fire and wood, and so resulting directly from the process. I was very focused on that idea at the time.

PM

They were very exciting days. We also moved the whole of your exhibition to St. Paul's Gallery in Leeds, including the soil, and then we brought it back and returned the soil to YSP. It was quite a tricky operation and it needed patience and commitment to be able to do it, but it was also interesting to be able to compare and contrast the indoors and the outdoors. Over a longer period of time, more of your work is exhibited indoors than outdoors.

DN

Yes, it's the nature of wood to decompose when left outside and I would say 90% of my work is shown indoors. I know you have more passion for sculpture in the open air than I do. I remember, for example, your Peter Randall-Page show, there were two fantastic granite forms in the Underground Gallery where my *Oculus Block* subsequently went, and I really loved them inside more than when they were outside. I mentioned it to you and you felt the reverse. For me, it's just a difference of

Opposite: *20 days with an Elm* worksite in 1981. Photographs: David Nash and YSP

opinion, but the things I make for outside, they are for outside.

PM
I have passion for sculpture, whether it's indoors or outdoors. To a certain extent in the early days, I had no option because we didn't have any indoors! So my passion was directed all the time to open-air spaces. I do enjoy placing works indoors that have been outdoors. One of the things I really like, and it took me a long time to get to that stage – mainly because of funding – is the indoor/outdoor relationship. I love that contrast. I think we've got one of the best galleries anywhere to work with both interior and exterior space.

It was fascinating recently to read your letter of application for the 1981 Fellowship again. You wrote that your work was to do with the environment and ecology and that this was the first consideration you had as an artist; also that you were concerned with enhancing rather than dominating. Ever since the very first exhibition at YSP, I've also been concerned with enhancing, though I wasn't aware of environmental and ecological issues to the extent that you were. You have taught us a great deal. Over the decades, have those early principles changed or been refined, have you struggled with them?

DN
The idea of just taking enough has always been important – that you just touch the wood enough to show the idea, or the human hand and the indication of the human being's intention, but not overdo it. It's partly because I'm so impatient, but I often found that what I had imagined I needed to do to a piece of wood was already there when I was only halfway to what I had originally imagined. To have gone further would have frozen it or killed it. The thing I've learned about trees is that they take only enough from their surroundings for their needs and they give back more. That is basically the answer to climate change: we have to give back more and take less.

PM
Your engagement with trees continues, but is that engagement any different now, because you don't do so much on-site working?

DN
From my time at YSP in the early 1980s through to the mid-1990s I often worked in situ at venues, but it was becoming a strain, and I couldn't take the work far enough in the limited amount of time that I was giving myself. I started actively looking for additional premises in Blaenau Ffestiniog, because I could afford it by then. I rented two units and then was able to buy them and then the land next to them, so I've been able to evolve studio and yard space. Before, I always went to the tree; now I'm bringing the tree to me. I can't do it on my own now, but that's because my body is failing me, but I've got the experience and I seem to be able to communicate in a friendly enough way for people to continue to come and help me saw. Also, we can take things further, because I can leave something I'm not sure about and go on with something else, and then usually it tells me the answer, because I've distanced myself, so I can come back to it.

PM
The way you're approaching it now is similar to the way that the marble carvers work in Pietrasanta and Carrara, where they need assistants to help them. The late Italian artist Giò Pomodoro used to refer to these people as the shadows of the great artists, which I think is a lovely way of putting it. I remember visiting you in California with Roger Evans when you were getting ready for your big show here, and you were working with Evan Shively on your *Oculus Block*.

DN
Yes, and Alan Smith also did chainsaw work

with me from around 1994 to 2004, and he travelled with me on projects. Evan Shively is a very good engineer and he's got a natural sense of how to make a saw to cut this massive piece of eucalyptus. Although they did have very long chainsaws, none of them would reach all the way through the trunk. You need to make one continual cut to get the right texture, without being muddled from cutting from one side and then from the other side. It took me a day to mark up for each cut, but it was done in one go with an enormous chainsaw with an engine at each end. Each cut took about half an hour.

PM
Can we move to the idea of the site-specific? Your work is, generally speaking, site-related.

DN
I like the word appropriate. Site-appropriate.

PM
Or site-generated?

DN
They are generated by the site, but being appropriate, that's also about the people who live and exist there.

PM
Would you say *Seventy-One Steps* that you made at YSP in 2010 was site-specific?

DN
Absolutely: and appropriate, and useful. The walk up the steps that used to be there, which were rotting, was unbelievably uncomfortable because of the erratic spacing, and one of Roger Evans' requirements of his exhibition sponsorship was that there should be a work made to stay in the landscape. I was delighted when you took up the idea of my remaking the steps. *Seventy-One Steps* also relates to the *Barnsley Lump* that I made here in 1982, because of the coal under the Bretton estate, which is not evident on the surface.

It's a beautiful landscape, but there are coal seams underneath and that was where the wealth of this estate came from. That's what the *Barnsley Lump* is there for and that's why there is an avalanche of coal coming down the slope, with the black steps in it.

PM
Seventy-One Steps is indeed a beautiful piece of site-specific or site-appropriate art. It really fits into the environment, it enhances the landscape and it has a function. It's very interesting when you start to talk about the purpose of art, the purpose of sculpture. To me there is purpose in aesthetics and that's part of the nature of art, and with your *Steps* there's a practical function as well in that they enable people to walk up to the woods. The steps are tempting, they draw people on and up. The piece works on so many different levels. Visually it's a beautiful shape and individually the steps have a compelling quality about them because of the way they've been charred. Slightly later, in 2013, you returned to make two more pieces for the landscape, which together with *Seventy-One Steps*, create a 'Nash triangle'.

DN
Yes, I was keen to have more work at the Sculpture Park because of how wonderfully it had developed. I also felt I owed you a planting piece because of the failure of the larch work in the 1980s.

PM
49 Square and *Black Mound* stand either side of the pathway around the lake and have an interesting visual and conceptual relationship to one another as well as to the surrounding landscape.

DN
Yes, the white trunks of the Himalayan birch trees and the charred oak forms relate to each other. Also, one is 'coming' or growing, and the other is in a pause of 'going', because it's

Above: *Barnsley Lump*, 1982.
Opposite: *Seventy-One Steps*, 2010. Photographs: Jonty Wilde

Top: *Black Mound*, 2013. Bottom: *49 Square*, 2013
Photographs: Jonty Wilde

being maintained but otherwise would rot back into the earth. I planted the first version of *49 Square* in 2001 on my hillside at Cae'n-y-Coed where the *Ash Dome* is sited. I had seen a plantation of birch in Hokkaido that had a very particular aura of benevolence and stillness that made a deep impression on me. Birches in that climate grow very slowly, the wood is like silk with a very dense close grain. Himalayan birch has a very white paper-like bark, much whiter than our common birch, and grows well in the European climate. At YSP there is sloping ground close to the lake that was wide enough to accommodate seven rows of seven birches, seven feet apart and close enough to the *Black Mound* site for there to be a physical and visual link. Each planting site has different features of nature. The soil is different for a start, and the amount of direct light and the strength of wind also affect the way trees form. The wind in particular has been much stronger and more persistent than I had anticipated at YSP, where the birches are struggling and have needed extra support for longer than the trees at Cae'n-y-Coed. I should have left the lower side branches on for longer for the trunks to thicken more before pruning. We are having to let a crown develop lower than intended. But that's the nature of growing 'form'; each circumstance is different. The trees are healthy and are developing in the way that is unique to the site.

PM
As a planted work, *49 Square* has an inherent requirement for ongoing long-term care and intervention. As you say, you've already had to adapt to the natural environment and its particularities, to allow the piece to develop in a way that corresponds with your intentions. In contrast, *Black Mound* had a big performance element and drama in its initial making, through the charring of the surface.

DN
The performance element you mention was the burning. A circular hole about 70cm deep was dug and the carved oak stumps placed in it, with the tallest positioned in the centre and decreasing in height outwards. A mass of kindling was stacked around each piece and set on fire. Enhancing the wind with leaf blowers, we controlled the heat to deeply char the surfaces of the stumps. There was quite a crowd to witness the event.

PM
It was a fantastic experience to be able to see the charring process taking place here on site rather than the completed work simply being transported here and installed. It further affirms its relationship to this place, as does the fact that coal appears again.

DN
I wanted to make the coal more of a feature and to have enough space between the charred stumps for visitors to be able to enter the sculpture. In that way *Black Mound* is different from the *Black Domes* that I have made where the charred parts are tight to each other. The day after the burning, the spaces between the stumps were filled with crushed coal, which both anchors the stumps in position and again refers to the coal seams under the Park. The coal, which was otherwise destined for coal-powered energy plants, was donated by British Coal who had also given the coal for *Seventy-One Steps*. Of course, since 2015 coal power is being phased out and currently there are only three active coal-fired power stations in the UK.

PM
I said at the start of this discussion that the way YSP has developed has, to an extent, kept pace with the way you've evolved. From humble beginnings, and in rural locations outside of the recognised art establishment, we have grown in parallel to reach significant audiences both nationally and internationally. Alongside this goes an unfading sense of place and being informed by the land you inhabit. There's no question we have learned

Top: *David Nash at Yorkshire Sculpture Park*, 2010: installation view at Longside Gallery
Bottom: *Oculus Block*, 2010 in the Underground Gallery. Photographs: Jonty Wilde

a huge amount from you. It seems you've learned from YSP too and I wonder what your observations are in terms of the way we've evolved.

DN
What I love particularly about YSP is that it's a wonderful example of how something can start as a seed, as an idea, and that somebody – and it would have to be somebody like yourself with your particular qualities – can make it grow. I always thought of YSP as running on a shoestring, which I think you might agree with, but you managed and you were resourceful. I was very impressed. It was like magic: working with so many aspects of culture to make something happen. I've always felt YSP was something that was growing, and it did grow extraordinarily. You had to beg and borrow and be allowed to use the land, and now YSP owns parts of the land. Longside was also an incredible addition, and the workshops as well, so that artists could make work there. But the biggest development was the building of the Underground Gallery. When YSP achieved that, to me it became the major European centre for sculpture.

PM
The Underground Gallery is beautiful and inherently practical, designed to show sculpture. Its glazed concourse, light-filled spaces, and the way you move through the building all constantly reinforce the relationship between indoors and outdoors, between the work and the landscape. Having that gallery ultimately enabled us to stage your major exhibition, a life statement, in 2010.

DN
You had been asking me to make an exhibition at YSP since the mid-90s and I had been stalling, waiting for the then imagined new galleries. It wasn't until the Underground Gallery was built and you had Longside Gallery and the YSP Centre that the indoor possibilities were coherent in relation to each other that I could really respond. You opened the Underground with a William Turnbull exhibition in 2005 and it was then that I properly started to prepare. I came over to YSP frequently then to 'learn' the spaces and the journey between them. The second show was James Turrell, when I discovered how versatile the new spaces were – something further demonstrated by Andy Goldsworthy's exhibition in 2007. Each time the gallery was made unique by the installation. It is entirely functional for sculpture and the architecture itself is not the statement, as it is with so many museums where exhibitions almost seem secondary to the buildings.

PM
You talk about the journey and coherence between indoor spaces, and that was incredibly important as your exhibition took place across four separate galleries, with works in the open air leading from the Park's entrance right across the valley to Longside Gallery. Everything was carefully choreographed to draw out relationships, so that a narrative unfurled.

DN
A selection of my earliest work, drawings and small sculptures from the later 1960s and the 1970s, was shown in the Garden Gallery, paired with the *Wooden Boulder* film and the first *Wood Quarry* in Maentwrog shown in the Bothy, both projects that began in the late 1970s. A row of 10 *Columns* led you to those galleries through the long corridor of the Centre. The meat of the show was inside and outside the Underground Gallery. The reception space was filled with offcuts and even the invigilators' desk was replaced with a very large slab of eucalyptus. I placed a freshly carved limewood *Crack and Warp Column* in the corridor that would get quite hot in the sun so the cracking and warping happened through the duration of the show. Alongside the massive *Oculus Block* in the first room was a selection of my finest pieces in the large

central space, followed by charred sculptures, and concluding with a display relating to my planting works. Over the valley, the cavernous space of Longside was filled with the contents of Capel Rhiw, complemented by loans from museums and collectors. A separate room was built for the drawings and charred pieces that were made in 2001 in response to the 9/11 attack in New York and had not been shown before. So much work went to YSP from Capel Rhiw that I took the opportunity to put in a much stronger floor in the main hall while it was empty.

PM
You mentioned the duration of the preparation process and that we had been talking about the possibility of a major exhibition at YSP for many years. Can you describe how you worked towards such an enormous undertaking, featuring well over 200 sculptures as well as works on paper.

DN
I needed time to produce the momentous show that I felt we could do together. It was a very big focus for a long time. In addition to many visits to the Park, virtually every project I did from 2005 onwards was directed in some way towards the YSP exhibition in 2010/11. I made a *Crack and Warp Wall* for the museum in Emden, and the *Red Sheaves* for Kunsthalle Mannheim – they didn't fund me, but I made work for them so it could ultimately come to YSP. The *King and Queen* in bronze commissioned by Frederick Meijer Gardens and Sculpture Park in Grand Rapids started the edition and we then had the second cast for the show here. I embarked on the next panel of the *Family Tree* and went through my work from as far back as art college, selecting pieces that would show the journey through early ideas and experiments to find my way to wood and trees and their language. I also made two five-week long working trips to Evan Shively's woodyard in Northern California, where you came to visit. Our show needed some big sculptures – that meant big wood and Evan had big wood that was ethically sourced from trees blown down by storms. Redwood and eucalyptus trunks were skinned, fumigated and sent across the Atlantic to YSP by shipping container.

PM
You used that wood to make new sculptures on site at YSP. I remember enjoying spending time watching you working over in the yard at Longside, including using chainsaws at height from a cherry picker to carve *Red Column*. That called to mind your making *Square Nest* in the early days, although now with much greater regard for health and safety!

DN
The containers were unloaded at Longside where Alan Smith and I carved *Red Column*, *Sliced Cedars*, and *Oculus Block*. I also made a piece from an enormous elm in North Wales that had died in the 1980s and remained standing until 2006 when it fell; it was 10 tons in weight. The carved elm and redwood trunk were sited together just outside Longside Gallery looking across the valley. They were clad with planks and charred to become *Big Black* and *Black Butt*. The fire was visible from the Centre and someone who was unaware of what we were doing called the fire brigade, but luckily they graciously accepted that it was a controlled fire. It was certainly a complex and eventful installation. Looking back, I did make the mistake of calling it my last show, instead of saying my most complete show! I realised subsequently that I actually do have a life afterwards: my life before YSP, and then my life following YSP.

PM
It's very interesting to hear that, David, because I feel that all the contact we've had over the years led to that big exhibition in 2010. Now, having reflected on and considered the significance of a connection that has developed over forty years, it seems fitting

that this new exhibition, *Full Circle*, will be my last at YSP before my retirement. It is also poignant that trees are its subject. The trees were the custodians of this landscape long before it became YSP and many will remain long beyond our lifetimes. There is a circularity, a cycle of coming and going. David, I'm very happy and proud that you have been such a significant part of my own journey and the journey of YSP, and that your works will remain here to continue to grow, to evolve and to be enjoyed by generations to come. Thank you.

Peter Murray (left) and David Nash at the opening of *David Nash at Yorkshire Sculpture Park* in 2010
Following double page: David Nash in his drawing studio, January 2022. Photographs: Jonty Wilde

On Drawing

"Idea" is the spark that ignites the desire to "make". An idea might emerge from seemingly nowhere, an unformed thought, from curiosity or just looking. Ideas have energy and demand to become form. I find making marks on paper the most immediate way to grasp the idea before it fades. The first marks, if true to the idea's impulse, will guide the rest of the drawing.

Early in my career I recognised that my mark making skills were very limited and that I had evolved a style that I imposed on whatever subject I was drawing. To remedy this, I challenged myself to abandon the style and learn the marks that the subject demanded. I went out walking with no drawing materials and looked for a subject, some group of random objects, a group of boulders or a view that sparked my interest. When I found one, I would look and work out its dynamics, what was it that excited me, look for its essential lines and shapes, was it tall or wide?

Then I would return home, cut 10 sheets of paper to the shape the subject suggested. I fitted these into a drawing board I had made that I could wear and have both hands free. I would also select the range of materials the subject seemed to need and return to its place. On the first papers I figured out the marks; lines and smudges, where a line started and its direction, how much pressure to apply and how fast or slow the line needed to be. A hard fine graphite line or a thick wax line or a smudging charcoal line.

By the fourth or fifth paper I started fitting the learned lines together and let the subject take over, trying not to tidy up or make more marks than was necessary, not let myself fuss over any sense of finish. With each paper I learnt more until all 10 papers were used up, then I would walk home. My eyes, now tuned, experienced real "seeing", everything seemed illuminated and often a new subject revealed itself. Back in the studio I would spread out the papers. It was usually the seventh or eighth group of marks that spoke most clearly. Each subject taught me more marks.

David Nash

Tree at Beaminster, 1980 (detail)

Full Circle: David Nash and Drawing

Sarah Coulson, Curator

Although known primarily as a sculptor, drawing is as constant and necessary in David Nash's practice as the trees it grows from. It represents a way of learning about and understanding his subject, responding to and recording the natural world, and finding form for abstract ideas. Despite its significance, it is rare to see Nash's drawing displayed in its own right, and *Full Circle* is the first museum exhibition since *Elements of Drawing* at Leeds Art Gallery in 1996 to do so. The incredibly rich variety in the artist's mark making manifests across works made in six different decades, encompassing fine graphite lines, thick charcoal strokes, bold swathes of pure pigment applied with cloth, and even soil smudged by hand onto paper. All reflect the great energy and passion of a uniquely skilled draughtsman.

The expansiveness of Nash's approach to his drawing technique is something that he consciously developed following a realisation in the early 1970s that he was "applying the same style of drawing to each and every subject".[1] In response, he challenged himself not simply to extend his mark making, but to reconsider the very act of looking at a subject and how this was translated via his gestures onto the paper, until his eyes were truly "tuned to seeing".[2] For Nash, the definition of "seeing" is not limited solely to visual perception, it goes hand in hand with sensing and expressing the energy, the life force, of the natural forms that are observed.

In the Weston Gallery at YSP, the exhibition concentrates on Nash's drawings of trees where this keenness of eye is palpable. Though predominantly drawn from life, these works are not topographical or directly descriptive of place, despite specific locations often being referenced in their titles. Wider landscape is only hinted at, if featured at all. With an almost-forensic eye, the artist pares back peripheral details, leaving a single tree or maybe a copse, but never a pastoral view. Negative space and the blank ground of the paper are always an active force within which a tree sits, as though for a portrait, front and centre. Each tree bears witness to its surroundings through the way in which it has grown, influenced by its microclimate: each is the nuanced product of its situation and is drawn as such.

For Nash, drawing is not sedentary or sedate, it is physical and vital. Pushing, pressing, smudging, scraping: he embodies forms and energy through gesture and says "whatever the method there's a truth for the hand to learn in the medium and a truth to the surface receiving it".[3] Immediacy is essential and drawing represents a rapid outlet for creativity, an antidote to the often-slow labour and heft of making sculpture. Nash describes himself as impatient, with his drawings usually produced quickly in one sitting rather than being returned to. The vigour and physicality of his process was captured in the film *Woodman* from 1978[4], which shows Nash wearing a specially made drawing board supported by a strap around his neck and back, resting on his torso to enable both hands to be free to draw simultaneously.

Many of the drawings in this exhibition were made outdoors, based on direct observations from nature and capturing a particular moment on a particular day. When done in the open air the process is active and chance-laden, and the elements have a direct hand in shaping the work, whether by wind blowing loose pigment or rain drops dispersing ink. This is just one way that his

Seeing an Oak, 1993 (detail)

drawing can be described as being both *of* and *from* its surroundings. At times, Nash also takes his materials directly from the environment in the form of earth, mud, grass, river water, or the fruits of trees, using them in situ to reflect the place of making, to introduce an element of unpredictability, and to add to the physical presence of the work.

In contrast, Nash describes the environment when drawing indoors as "neutral". The resultant works are more reflective, ideas-based and not taken from life; they are made in his dedicated drawing studio, a former shop converted so that natural light floods in. Falling into this family are drawings that capture and give form to a feeling or characteristic such as colour, so vibrantly demonstrated in *Red Tree* (2021) [page 56], which is one of an ongoing series of imagined trees in this intense hue. There is a velvety softness to these strokes that could not be achieved through the direct use of pastels on paper, but is created instead by loading powdered pigment onto a fleece pad before applying it; a perfect example of Nash searching to find a technique that most precisely expresses his intention.

In Nash's practice, drawing and sculpture exist in a symbiotic relationship, examining many of the same fundamental themes. However, drawing on paper is not part of his process of developing sculpture, and for this he relies on a different and somewhat unconventional approach. As though working through a mathematical formula, he draws onto a blackboard to help him search for latent forms within the wood that has become available to him. He says: "as well as the chainsaw, chalk and a blackboard have been crucial for the making of my sculpture".[5] These visual calculations are not kept for posterity as they would be in the pages of a sketchbook, but are quickly wiped away with a board rubber ready for the next, their contribution evident only in the evolving sculptural outcome. The momentary nature of this method does not compromise or too rigidly dictate the artist's need to follow the idiosyncrasies of the timber as he carves, rather it is a way to guide his hand and thinking.

When Nash does make drawings of his sculpture on paper, it is in a retrospective or documentary capacity. *Frêne* (1988) [page 48] in the Weston Gallery is such a work, and relates to the *Chêne et Frêne* (Oak and Ash) wood quarry that he undertook at the 12th-century Tournus Abbey at Pierre-de-Bresse in France. Green watercolour depicts the shape of the ash tree as it grew and, like a butchery diagram, mapped over the top of it in yellow are the individual sections of the tree that he went on to use in the creation of particular sculptures; for example, the main part of the trunk near the base and the lowest right-hand branch became one half of *Two Ubus* (1988). *Frêne* illustrates how sculptural shapes are engendered by the growth patterns of the tree, and visually demonstrates the concept of the wood quarry: "I follow their veins, shapes and volumes to find forms that echo their character and story, giving it voice".[6]

Vastly different in character are the wood quarry drawings on display in the Bothy Gallery that were made during Nash's 1981-82 YSP Fellowship, when for the first time he was able to work on one tree for a sustained three-week period rather than returning to it sporadically over two years as he had with his first quarries at Maentwrog and Tan-y-Bwlch in North Wales. The associated drawings betray the distilled energy and intensity of the YSP worksite, frenetic and alive with new ideas, a laboratory for real-time research. Working directly with the process of making sculpture was a key notion and Nash experimented with relinquishing control in order to pursue unpredictable results, for example *Scorch Δ I* (1981) [page 64] was made by setting a fire within a hollowed-out trunk and laying paper over the top of the triangular cavity for long enough to allow it to scorch the sheet. Such drawings act as markers of a fleeting moment in the life of an evolving sculptural work as well as being works in their own right.

The ultimate expression of the artist's surveying and documenting previous sculptures through drawing is his remarkable *Family Tree*, a series of large-scale graphic works that traces the many and complex conceptual and formal relationships between his three-dimensional oeuvre. Small but incredibly evocative drawings are connected together by charcoal lines that reveal the traces and paths of ideas and influence. Gem-like, these miniature ciphers are rendered so deftly that there can be no doubt of the often-monumental pieces to which they relate. This ability comes not only from skill in drawing but from a profound haptic knowledge of the finest subtleties of all his sculptures, a knowledge that translates through motion and gesture into the drawing material. In this exhibition, *Family Tree* is represented, unusually, by an etching of 1981 [page 70], produced at the Yorkshire Print Makers Workshop whilst Nash was resident at YSP during his Fellowship year and later updated with drawings of the works he produced at the Park in 1982, including the planted piece *Three Stones for Three Trees* [pages 82-83] that still grows here.

Another principal branch of the artist's two-dimensional work is the careful and exhaustive chronicling of the development of his growing or "coming" works, especially the iconic *Ash Dome* (1977), which he has been drawing regularly for 45 years. Spanning manifold styles and types of mark making, this large and evolving group could be seen as a microcosm of his graphic work as a whole and reveals a rare dedication to medium, subject and challenging a uniform way of seeing. The drawings range from detailed studies, almost like annotated botanical diagrams, documenting how the work was physically planted, pruned and nurtured – with notes such as "first fletch", "pruning to stimulate vertical growth", "new branches stimulated by bending over" – through to abstract domes of vibrant pure colour that capture a more spiritual quality. *Ash Dome* as an entity remains constant, but at times it is portrayed as dark and brooding, and at others light and ethereal, affected by weather, time of day or year, but also by how the artist perceives its aura at any given moment. This approach is also embodied in the drawings produced at the Royal Botanic Gardens, Kew, where a residency in 2012-13 made it possible for Nash to observe specimen trees, including the ancient weeping beech, through the seasons: "in winter I could study its structure… the spring and summer leaves transformed the tree into a display of vibrant energy".[7]

The *Ash Dome* drawing in this exhibition, from 2007 [pages 46-47], uses soil from the ground where the work grows as a material, and was made by "pushing charcoal through the earth in an upwards growing gesture"[8], echoing its life force. Insinuating the experience of the environment onto the page is similarly epitomised by the beautiful *Autumn Leaves in a River, November, Llan Ffestiniog* (1983) [page 40]. Walking by a river in autumn, Nash noticed the huge number of leaves moving and swirling in the flow of water. This sparked an excitement to find a way of making an image from this continual movement. When he returned several days later, he was at first disappointed to find far fewer leaves in the water, but realised that he could only draw one leaf at a time so the new situation became an advantage. Each time a leaf floated by, he drew it using ink and then dipped his paper into the river to partially dissolve the mark. Repeating the process with each new leaf that drifted past, he gradually built up the drawing: the earliest leaves he had drawn became barely visible, just showing a trace of their outline, whereas the later ones remained stronger and clearer. Working in this way enabled Nash to capture the memory of a fleeting period of time and share this experience in his drawing. *Autumn Leaves* embodies the artist's approach to drawing what he sees in the moment, using experimental techniques, working quickly, and setting up situations where the natural environment takes an active role in the creation of artwork.

One of the most striking recent developments in Nash's drawing is a return to colour and an increased level of abstraction, albeit in the paring back and condensing of themes and subjects from the natural world. His fascination for colour, and theories related to its formal, spatial and emotional properties, stems from his original studies as a painter, when he was looking to artists such as Arshile Gorky and Wassily Kandinsky. A longstanding interest in Rudolf Steiner also feeds into his absorption in ideas around the spiritual qualities of different colours and how they speak to the human soul by arousing distinct psychological responses. When he moved away from painting canvas, colour became a dominant factor in Nash's earliest sculptural works, and he painted wooden structures in bold, often primary, hues. However, he soon became dissatisfied with applied colour that was not integral to the material and seemed to him like an "artificial skin"[9] sitting on the surface and obscuring the character of the wood. Subsequent experiments with staining fell short for the same reasons. Nash describes this juncture, which took him down a decisive path: "I abandoned my colour requirement and accepted the natural colour of the supporting material I had been using – wood – which in itself became a teacher and I followed where it led. Nonetheless, the vibrant life of pure colour has continued to be important to me".[10]

The colour red, which lately finds such potent expression in the *Red Trees* drawings, has long been of consequence in his oeuvre, and occurs naturally in the wood of a number of trees used by the artist: the central Underground Gallery space for his 2010 YSP exhibition housed the towering redwood *Red Sheaves* (2008), the deep-toned sequoia *Red Frame* (2008), and the warm yew of *Red Flash* (2003). In the early 1990s he began to extend its use in graphic work, inspired by the symbolism of its combination with black and white: "Red, black and white are a potent triad significant in many cultures and legends. In the search for the Holy Grail there is a description of a crow [black] shot by an arrow lying bleeding [red] in the snow [white]. To explore the potential of this triad I turned to pigment on paper".[11]

This move into pigment gained momentum and began to draw on a wider range of colours taken directly from the landscape. *Oak Leaves Through May* (2016) [page 58] is described by Nash as an "observation colour drawing" because its origin was a series of colours he discovered in nature. Over the course of a month, he took careful note of oak tree leaves emerging from their buds, noticing their gradual growth and evolving tones: "In May of 2016 I watched more closely the oaks coming into leaf. At first the trees have an amber ambience when the leaves are very small. As they grow that amber lightens to a yellow, then, as the chlorophyll starts to form, a light green and then to a darker green with a wax surface when the leaves are fully functioning".[12] The artist rendered this barely perceptible, gradual transformation into a large-scale, bold abstract work comprising stacked rectangles of pure colour. From a distance, each block appears solid and uniform, but on closer inspection it is apparent that the pigment has been applied by hand to build up these intense hues through layering.

In 2020, Nash took this concept still further in a series of "colour mood" drawings based on his sensory experience of the seasons, and which he described as "the first time for me to enter such an abstract endeavour".[13] As colours change in the landscape through the year when different plants, shrubs and trees are in foliage and flower, they create visual colour rhythms:

May and *July* (both 2020) [page 58] capture the dominant colour tones that the artist observed during those months. Using circular motions of pigment-coated pads, he forms orbs, decreasing the pressure applied towards the outside of each circle to create the sense of a halo, of a form emerging from the page. Finding the right relationship between the colours to enable them to "make visual music",[14] involves using cut circles of each colour and moving them around on a blank sheet until the balance is achieved and the piece sings, at which point the final drawing is made. Such a process indubitably draws on the artist's abiding fascination for colour theory, whether colours are regressive or dominant, calm or active, how they harmonise; connecting back to and boldly revitalising ideas that first found expression in his work over fifty years ago.

Yorkshire Sculpture Park's relationship with David Nash has evolved across six decades and each of those is represented by drawings in this exhibition, including several that use the very earth from the ground beneath our feet. It is fitting that this selection of works references the cycles of nature, the passing of time as marked and measured in the seasonal changes that set the tempo of the natural world around us. Bursting into life and leaf, or returning slowly back to the earth. Reminding us of our mortality. Coming full circle.

Endnotes

1. David Nash, in a film made about his drawing for YSP in 2022
2. Ibid.
3. David Nash, 'Lines and Smudges' in Nicholas Thornton ed., *David Nash: Two Hundred Seasons at Capel Rhiw*. Cardiff, National Museum of Wales, 2019, p97
4. *Woodman*, 1978, Arts Council of Great Britain, Director Peter Francis Browne
5. David Nash, in a film made about his drawing for YSP in 2022
6. David Nash, in *David Nash: The Many Voices of Trees*. Paris: Galerie Lelong & Co., p9
7. David Nash, in a film made about his drawing for YSP in 2022
8. Ibid.
9. David Nash on *Blue Ring* in Marina Warner, *David Nash: Forms in Time*. London: Academy Editions, 1996, p108
10. Ibid.
11. David Nash in Hugh Aldersay-Williams, *David Nash: Wood, Metal, Pigment*. London: Annely Juda Fine Art, 2018, p83
12. Ibid.
13. David Nash, cited on www.galleriesnow.net/shows/david-nash-trees-2/ [accessed 19 March 2022]
14. Ibid.

Following double page: *Red Tree*, 2021 (detail)

The Weston Gallery

Lines and Smudges

Marks on paper, lines and smudges, an idea looking for a form or just a notion needing clarity, a fine graphite line, a thick charcoal line, a cloth pad loaded with pigment. Whatever the method there's a truth in the medium for the hand to learn and a truth in the surface receiving it.

David Nash

Burnt Trees, 1980 (detail)

Making Marks with the Subject's Material

To make a drawing more connected to the subject I look to see if the subject's actual material could be used. With *Ash Dome* the earth from which it grows can be a starting point. Scraping up a handful of the leaf mould and earth and rubbing it into the paper then drawing through the debris with charcoal with an upward growth gesture, then shaking off the dirt to see what I have got and continue from there. Drawing the planting of a group of small saplings I would first rub the paper in the dirt to make a "ground" as a starting point. Drawing leaves moving in the current of a river I tried immersing the ink drawing in the river to see how this might enhance the image. Drawing brambles using the fruit squashed into the paper. The point of this is to loosen the sense of "picture" and allowing the unexpected to be an essential part of what happens on the paper.

David Nash

Autumn Leaves in a River, November, Llan Ffestiniog, 1983
Following page: *Blackthorns, Harlech Dome*, 1979

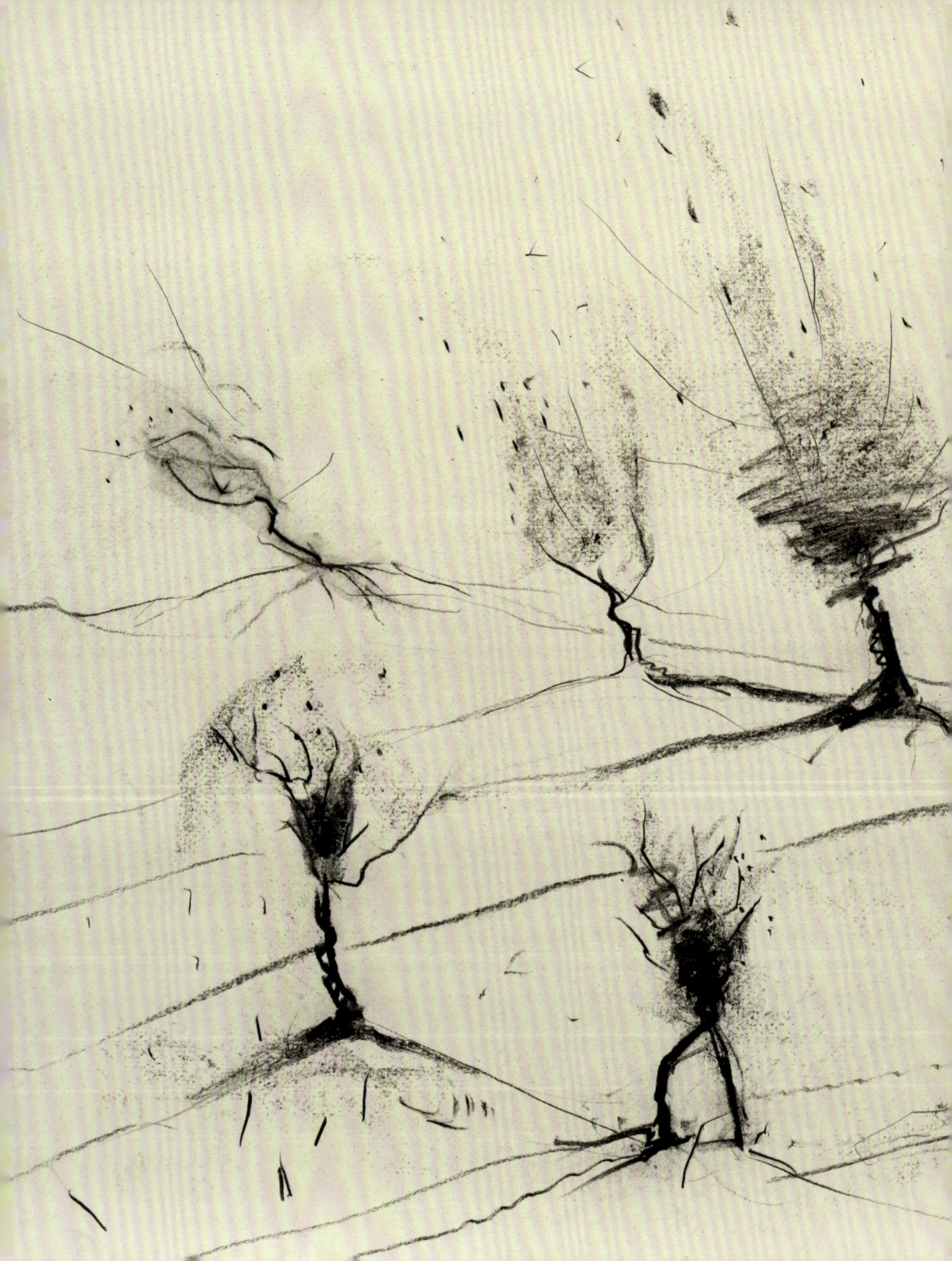

Opposite: top to bottom, left to right: *Seeing an Oak*, 1993; *Spruce and Larch*, 1992; framed together – *Ski Run Larches*, 1992, *Larches in Snow, France*, 1992, and *Larches in Snow*, 1992; *Tree at Beaminster*, 1980; *Cae'n-y-Coed*, 1980; *Shapes of Shade, Brittany*, 1983. Following pages, left, top to bottom: *Ash Seeds*, 2013; *Ash Dome*, 2007; right, *Ash Dome*, 2007 (detail)

Working with Trees

Planting and nurturing live trees, carving and honing dead trees, I learn better how to behave in the environment we share.

Trees have a life resembling our own, they communicate with others and have a social life. They work to thrive, trading in the soil with fungi, sugars for mineral, and trade in the air, oxygen for carbon dioxide. This subtle economy enables them to build resilient bodies and to propagate and at the same time enrich the environment. They take just enough and give back more.

In life they stand balanced, spreading, defiant, weaving the elemental forces of light, warmth, water, earth and air into their material bodies. Essentially they are fully alive to their environment.

In death they surrender to insects and fungi that live on and in them. Their activity takes the tree back into the ground, reintegrating it as humus. At all stages, trees and wood speak their place and progress in this great cycle of coming and going, soaked in weather and time.

For sculpture I only use trees that have become naturally available at the end of their lives. These trees become a wood quarry for me. Often working where they fell I follow their veins, shapes and volumes to find forms that echo their character and story, giving it voice.

David Nash

Opposite: *Frêne*, 1988
Following double page: installation view

Opposite, left column: *Olive, Barontoli*, 2001.
Right column, top to bottom: *Two Olives, Sienna*, 2001;
Olive, Sienna, 2001; *Olive, Sienna*, 2001
Following double page: installation view

Above: *Red Tree, 2021*. Opposite, top: *Three Twmp Tops, 2000*; bottom: *Inside a Twmp*, 2000
Following double page, left to right: *May*, 2020; *July*, 2020; *Oak Leaves Through May*, 2021

The Bothy Gallery

Previous page: *West Bretton Δs and Ys*, 1981 (detail)
Above: *Felled Elm, Bretton*, 1981. Opposite: *Pyramid and Mould*, 1981 (detail)
Following page, left to right: *Scorch Δ I*, 1981; *Δ Brushwood Ash – Elm*, 1981; *Pile of Vs*, 1981

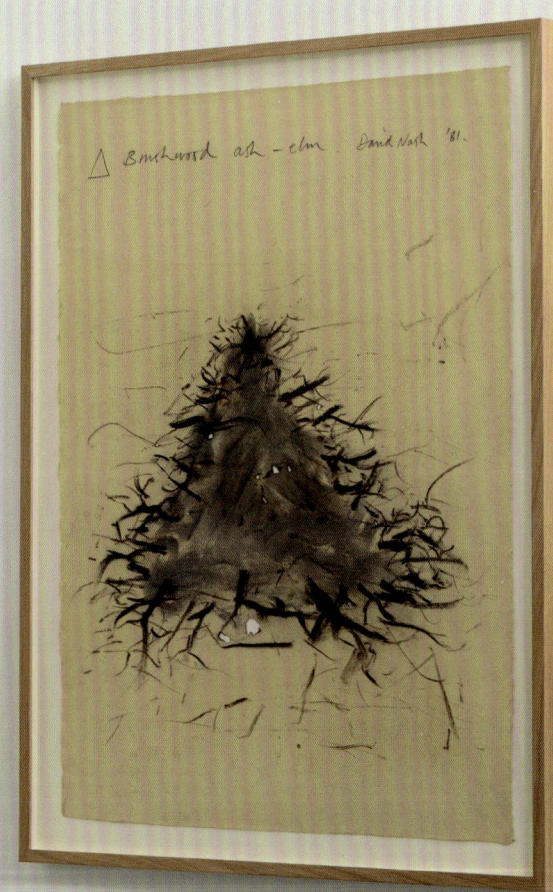

Above: worksite at YSP, 1981. Opposite: *Pyramids and Catapults, 20 Days with an Elm*, 1981
Following page: *Wood Quarry* Δ, 1981

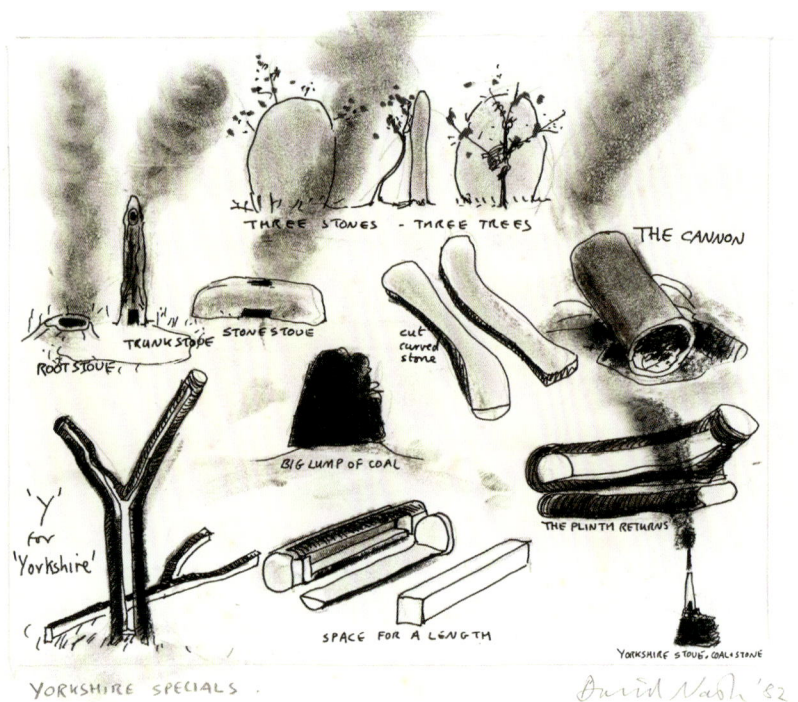

Top: *Yorkshire Specials*, 1982. Bottom: *Family Tree*, 1982. Opposite: *Root Stove and Trunk Stove*, 1982

Wood Quarry, Otterlo, 1982

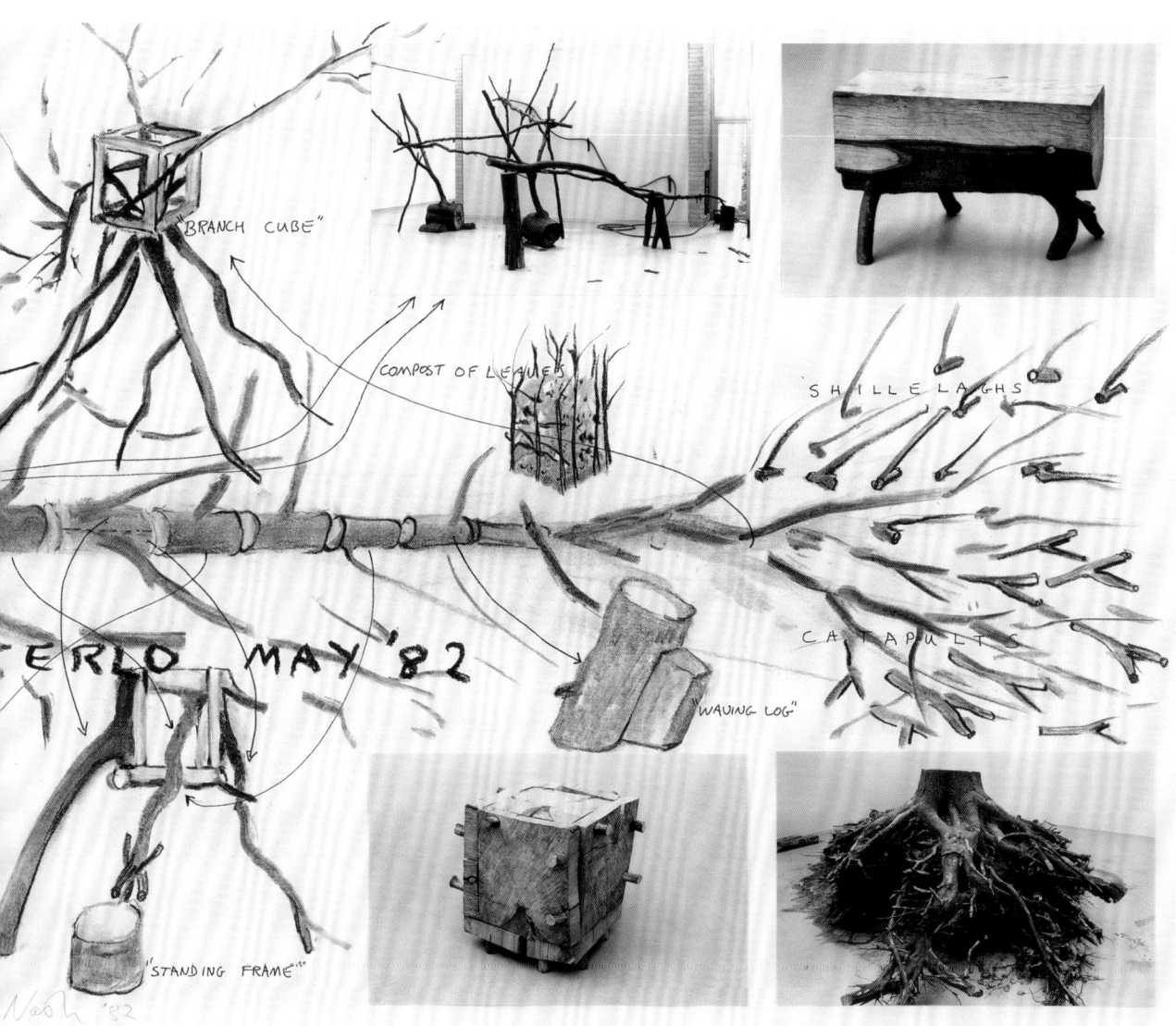

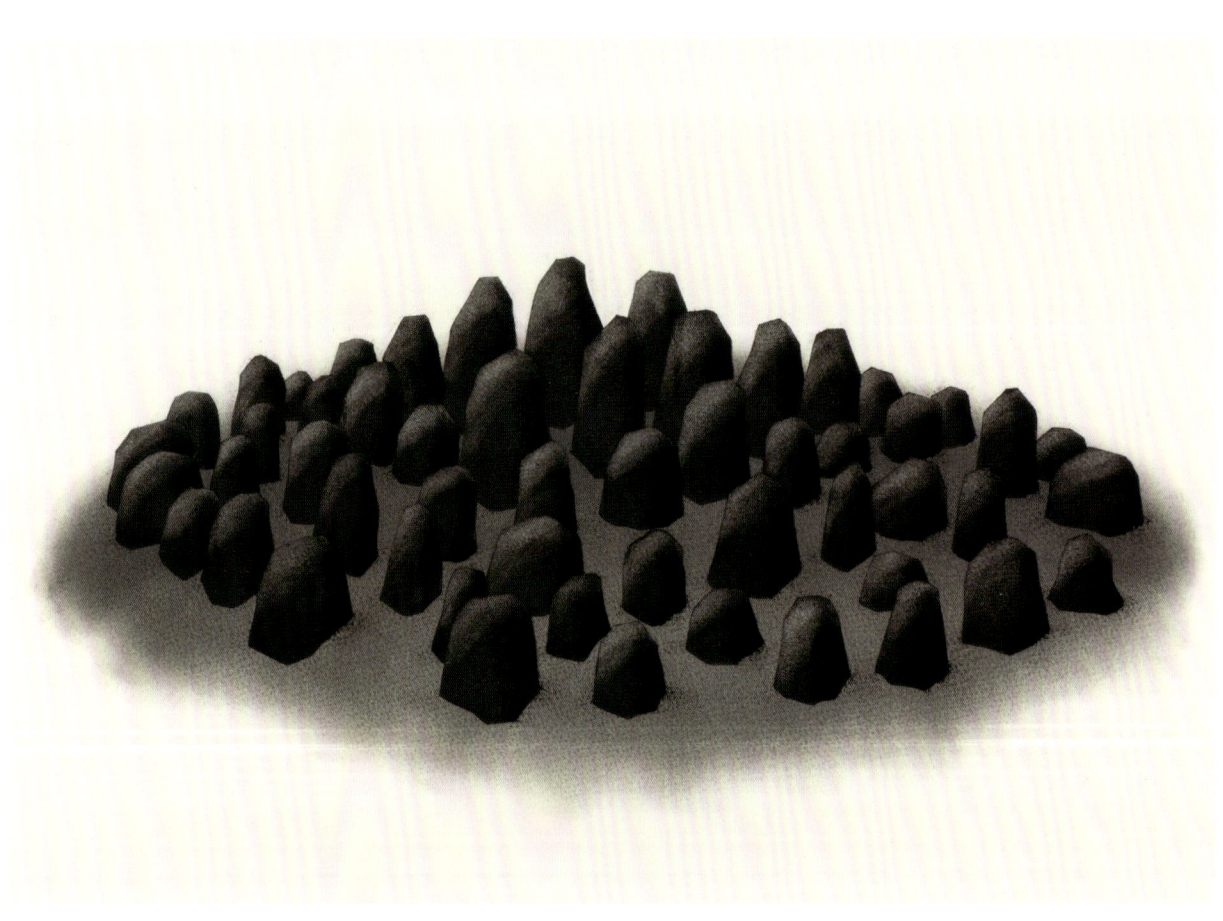

Above: *Black Mound*, 2021. Photograph: Red Photography
Opposite: *49 Square*, 2013 (detail). Following page: blackboard drawing showing all Nash's projects at YSP, made in 2022 for this exhibition

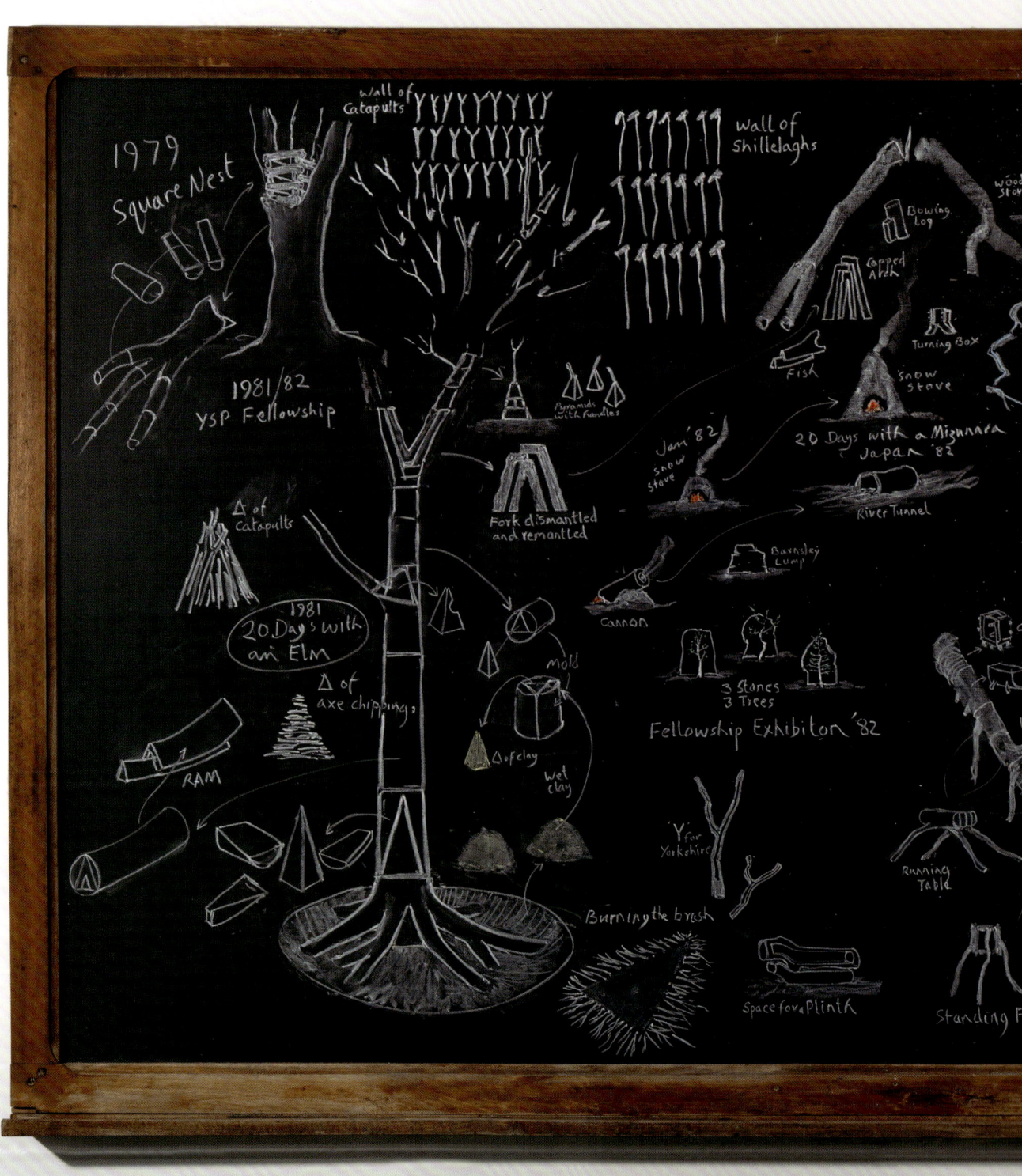

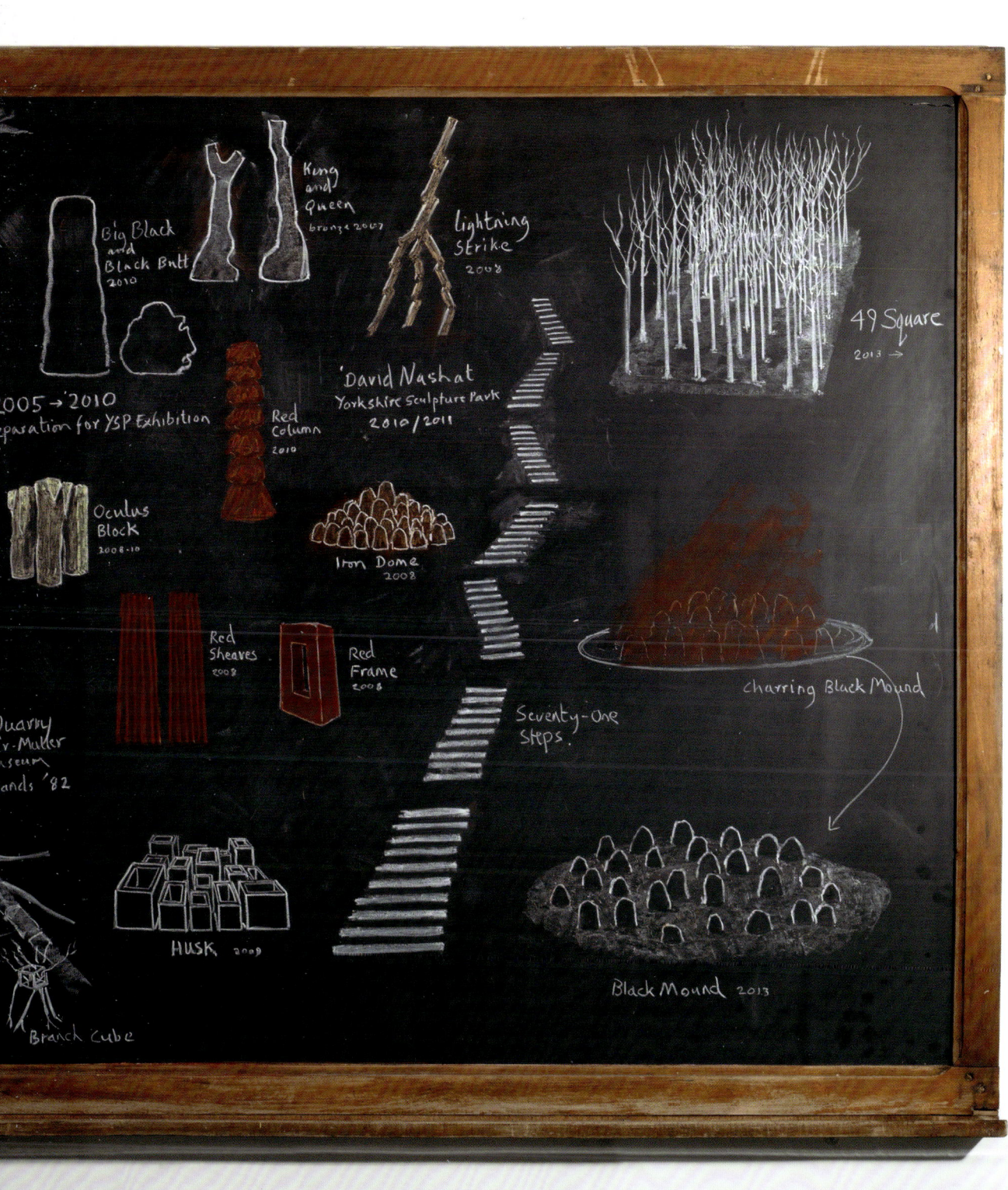

Pages 78-79: Nash burning *Black Trunk, Black Butt* at YSP in 2010
Pages 80-81: Nash carving with a chainsaw at YSP in 2010
Above: *Three Stones for Three Trees*, 1982, taken in 1982
Opposite: *Three Stones for Three Trees*, 1982, taken in 2022

List of Works

20 Days with a Mizunara, 1982
Charcoal on paper
38.5 x 95 cm

49 Square, 2013
Pastel, chalk and graphite on paper
70 x 100 cm

Apple and Yew, Plas Tan-yr-Allt, 1989
Charcoal on paper
59 x 80 cm

Ash Dome, 2007
Earth and charcoal on paper
56.5 x 76 cm

Ash Seeds, 2013
Charcoal and pastel on paper
91 x 63 cm

Autumn Leaves in a River, November, Llan Ffestiniog, 1983
Ink and river water on paper
56 x 75.5 cm

Big Beech Going at Space, 1978
Graphite on Japanese paper
93 x 63 cm

Big Beech, Pen-y-Mount, 1978
Graphite on Japanese paper
93 x 63 cm

Black Mound for YSP, 2013
Charcoal and pastel on paper
70 x 100 cm

Blackthorns, Harlech Dome, 1979
Graphite and charcoal on paper
45.5 x 63 cm

Box of Trees, 1983
Charcoal on paper
57 x 76 cm

Δ *Brushwood Ash – Elm*, 1981
Charred stick ash on paper
79 x 57.5 cm

Budding Leaves, 1981
Charcoal and graphite on paper
45 x 59 cm

Burnt Trees, 1980
Charcoal on paper
56 x 76 cm

Cae'n-y-Coed, 1980
Bracken char and charcoal on paper
52 x 64 cm

Cherry, Spring, Kew, 2012
Charcoal and eraser on paper
56 x 76 cm

Chestnut Leaved Oak, Kew, 2012
Charcoal on paper
76 x 57 cm

Chestnut Leaved Oak, Kew, 2012
Charcoal on paper
76 x 57 cm

Copse, Bangor, Minffordd, 1979
Charcoal and earth on paper
58 x 79 cm

Crossing, Closed and Open, 1982
Graphite and ink on paper
46 x 51 cm

Family Tree, 1982
Etching
74 x 91 cm

Felled Elm, Bretton, 1981
Charcoal, graphite and wax on paper
56 x 76 cm

Four Pines on a Dutch Hill, Otterlo, 1979
Graphite and wax on paper
58 x 79 cm

Four Stages of a Mature Redwood, 1987
Charcoal on paper
Four elements, each 48 x 64 cm

Frêne, 1988
Watercolour on paper
120 x 90 cm

Horse Chestnut, Amsterdam, 1981
Wax on paper
64 x 52 cm

Inside a Twmp, 2000
Charcoal on paper in charred frame
100 x 151 cm

July, 2020
Pastel on paper
153.5 x 102.5 cm

Larches in Snow, 1992
Charcoal on paper
17 x 25 cm

Larches in Snow, France, 1992
Charcoal on paper
17 x 25 cm

May, 2020
Pastel on paper
153 x 102.5 cm

Oak Leaves Through May, 2021
Pigment on paper
Five elements, each 48 x 121 cm

Olive, Barontoli, 2001 (1)
Pastel on paper
25 x 35 cm

Olive, Barontoli, 2001 (2)
Pastel on paper
25 x 35 cm

Olive, Barontoli, 2001 (3)
Pastel on paper
25 x 35 cm

Olive, Barontoli, 2001 (4)
Pastel on paper
25 x 35 cm

Olive, Sienna, 2001 (1)
Charcoal and eraser on paper
42 x 59 cm

Olive, Sienna, 2001 (2)
Charcoal and eraser on paper
42 x 59 cm

Pile of Vs, 1981
Elm
65 x 52 x 46 cm

Pyramid and Mould, 1981
Earth, charcoal and graphite on paper
52 x 72 cm

Pyramid of Axe Chips, 1981
Charcoal on paper
50 x 46 cm

Pyramid on Legs, 1981
Elm
62 x 32 x 34 cm

Pyramid with Handle, 1981
Elm
52 x 28 x 18 cm

Pyramid with Handle, 1981
Elm
38 x 17 x 15 cm

Pyramids and Catapults,
20 Days with an Elm, 1981
Charcoal, earth and wax on paper
137 x 82.5 cm

Red Tree, 2021
Pastel on paper
122 x 110 cm

Scorch Δ I, 1981
Wood smoke and ash on paper
55 x 45 cm

Seeing an Oak, 1993
Charcoal on paper
46 x 60 cm

Shapes of Shade, Brittany, 1983
Graphite on paper
51 x 63.5 cm

Ski Run Larches, 1992
Charcoal on paper
17 x 25 cm

Spruce and Larch, 1992
Charcoal on paper
59 x 42 cm

Square Nest, 1979
Charcoal on paper, and photograph
73 x 110 cm

Sweet Chestnut, Kew, March, 2012 (1)
Charcoal on paper
57 x 76 cm

Sweet Chestnut, Kew, March, 2012 (2)
Charcoal on paper
57 x 76 cm

Three Twmp Tops, 2000
Pastel on paper in charred frame
74.5 x 100 cm

Tree at Beaminster, 1980
Graphite and chalk on paper
30 x 55 cm

Turner's Oak, Kew, 2012
Charcoal on paper
57 x 76 cm

Two Olives, Sienna, 2001
Charcoal and eraser on paper
42 x 59 cm

Untitled, Amsterdam, 1981
Graphite on paper
64 x 52 cm

Weeping Beech, Kew, 2012 (1)
Pastel on paper
67 x 102 cm

Weeping Beech, Kew, 2012 (2)
Pastel on paper
67 x 102 cm

Weeping Beech, Kew, 2012 (3)
Pastel on paper
67 x 102 cm

Weeping Beech, Kew, March, 2012
Charcoal on paper
67 x 102 cm

West Bretton Δs and Ys, 1981
Earth, charcoal, and pastel on paper
56 x 76 cm

Wood Quarry II, Tan-y-Bwlch, 1981
Charcoal and fire brash on paper
76.5 x 56 cm

Wood Quarry, Otterlo, 1982
Charcoal on paper
38 x 95 cm

Wood Quarry Δ, 1981
Earth, charcoal and graphite on paper
123.5 x 182.5 cm

Yorkshire Specials, 1982
Charcoal on paper
19 x 24 cm

David Nash and Gordon Young
Untitled, 1979
Graphite, earth and charcoal on paper
57 x 76 cm

David Nash and Paul Neagu
Ring of Trees, Otterlo (David Nash);
Definition (Paul Neagu), 1979
Charcoal, graphite and gesso on paper
56.5 x 76 cm

Colophon

Published to accompany
DAVID NASH: FULL CIRCLE

Weston and Bothy Galleries,
Yorkshire Sculpture Park
19 February 2022 to 5 June 2022

ISBN 978-1-908432-56-8

Exhibition photography
Jonty Wilde

Book design / production
Sarah Coulson

Proofreading
Louise Lohr
Helen Pheby

Print
Jump (North), Sheffield

© the authors and Yorkshire Sculpture Park 2022. All rights reserved. No part of this publication may be reproduced, stored in a retrieval system or transmitted in any form or by any means without the prior permission in writing of the publisher.